Modern DRUM STUDIES

A Series of Carefully-Conceived Exercises for the Snare Drum and Bass Drum

SIMON STERNBURG

Foreword

Modern Drum Studies by Simon Sternburg consists of a series of carefully conceived exercises for the snare drum and bass drum.

Through his extensive knowledge of percussion playing, Mr. Sternburg realized the necessity for a work of this kind and devoted a great deal of time and thought in preparing and designing these exercises for both the student and advanced player. Of course, it is assumed that the student has had some previous instruction in notation before commencing these exercises—reading of which is a prime requisite.

Simon Sternburg was one of America's leading percussionists, with an extremely interesting background. As a member of the Boston Symphony Orchestra, he played under some of the most celebrated conductors in the world, including the great Koussevitsky. He also played with name Latin-American bands.

For many years, Mr. Sternburg taught the art of drumming at the Boston University College of Music. However, it was while editing a column for "Metronome" that he had exceptional opportunities for discovering the involved problems of the student. As a result of the knowledge gained thereby, the present work was undertaken.

Thus, *Modern Drum Studies,* by the very capable and experienced Simon Sternburg, has become a "must" wherever percussion instruments are taught.

The Publisher

About this Revised Edition

Modern Drum Studies by Simon Sternburg has become a classic with all snare drum teachers who are concerned with developing their student's reading skills. Originally published in 1933, Mr. Sternburg sought to fill a tremendous need in percussion instruction. At that time, there were very few books on Latin-American rhythm instruments and various traps such as temple blocks and timpani. Today there are many excellent books which focus entirely on those areas. In this revised edition of *Modern Drum Studies*, we have deleted those pages and have kept all of the core materials for reading development of snare drum and bass drum.

The overwhelming amount of letters and phone calls from teachers *demanding* that this book remain available as part of the core literature for percussion instruction, has motivated Alfred to republish the classic snare drum publication in revised form.

We hope all of you learn and grow from it, as was Simon Sternburg's goal in his original creation in the 1930s.

RHYTHMIC STUDIES

For
Snare Drum and Bass Drum

*"R" Indicates right stick; "L" Indicates left stick.   Begin even groups of notes with right stick.

** Begin roll with left stick.   Begin uneven groups with left stick.

"R" Indicates right stick; "L" Indicates left stick.

Begin roll with left stick.

Begin even groups of notes with right stick.

Begin uneven groups with left stick.

"R" Indicates right stick; "L" Indicates left stick.
   Begin roll with left stick.
Begin even groups of notes with right stick.
Begin uneven groups with left stick.

"R" Indicates right stick; "L" Indicates left stick.

Begin roll with left stick.

Begin even groups of notes with right stick.

Begin uneven groups with left stick.

"R" Indicates right stick; "L" Indicates left stick.

Begin roll with left stick.

Begin even groups of notes with right stick.

Begin uneven groups with left stick.

Raise stick high for accented notes.

42

43

24

30

34

100

101 FAST

54

55

121

122

* To simplify counting divide measure into triplets as follows
① Exactly same as first measure.

as written

as played.

as written

as played.

123 in Four

~ see preceding exercise ~

Group of five notes are single stroke: and not a five stroke roll.